Cities through Time

Daily Life in
Ancient and Modern

by Robert F. Baldwin

illustrations by Ray Webb

RP

Runestone Press/Minneapolis
A Division of the Lerner Publishing Group

The *Cities through Time* series is produced by Runestone Press, a division of the Lerner Publishing Group, in cooperation with Greenleaf Publishing, Inc., Geneva, Illinois.

Text design by Melanie Lawson
Cover design by Michael Tacheny

The Lerner Publishing Group
241 First Avenue North
Minneapolis, Minnesota 55401

Website address: www.lernerbooks.com

Library of Congress Cataloging-in-Publication Data

Baldwin, Robert F.
    Daily life in ancient and modern Beijing / by Robert F. Baldwin ;
illustrations by Ray Webb.
        p.   cm. — (Cities through time)
    Includes index.
    Summary: Explores daily life in Beijing in both ancient and modern
times.
    ISBN: 0–8225–3214–X (lib. bdg. : alk. paper)
    1. Peking (China)—Social life and customs—Juvenile literature.
[1. Peking (China)—Social life and customs.]   I. Webb, Ray, ill.
II. Title.   III. Series.
DS795.2.B35   1999
951'.156—DC21   98–17769

Manufactured in the United States of America
1 2 3 4 5 6 – JR – 04 03 02 01 00 99

Contents

Introduction 4

ANCIENT BEIJING

The Earliest Inhabitants 6

A Military Outpost 8

A Royal Household 10

Peasants, Merchants, and Artisans 12

A Slave's Life 14

The Khitans and Yenjing 16

Walls and Invaders 18

IMPERIAL BEIJING

Life Under Kublai Khan 20

A Man Named Marco 22

Forbidden City 24

The Lives of Women 26

The Mandarin Exam 28

Kites and Games 30

Offering Sacrifices 32

When People Got Sick 34

Tai Chi Chuan and the Art of Combat 36

Singers with Painted Faces 38

The Empire Slowly Crumbles 40

MODERN BEIJING

An Occupied City 42

The Walls Come Down 44

Events in Tiananmen Square 46

Life in a Crowded City 48

Rivers of Bicycles 50

Language and School 52

Eating in Beijing 54

New Year! 56

Life Goes On 58

Beijing Timeline 60

Books about China and Beijing 62

Index 63

About the Author and Illustrator 64

Introduction

Beijing, the capital of China, is so old, there are no records of when it began. Yet we know it already existed 3,000 years ago. In ancient times, the city on the site of modern Beijing was a trading outpost near the northern edge of China. To the south was a vast area where most of China's people lived and farmed. To the north were mountains. Beyond those lay the plains of Mongolia, where nomadic peoples made their homes. Some Mongol groups formed raiding parties that invaded Chinese lands.

In the city's early days, China was not yet a single nation. The Chinese people belonged to small kingdoms that fought against one another or against Mongol raiders. Located near the frontier, Beijing needed a strong army to defend itself in case of attack.

When attackers were successful, the new ruler would often rename the city. Throughout the centuries, Beijing has also been called Chi, Yenjing, Khanbalik, Peiping, and Peking.

In addition to being governed by outsiders, the city became the capital of various Chinese emperors who built many imperial palaces and other royal structures. Except for two periods—from 1368 to 1421 and from 1928 to 1949, when the capital was moved to Nanjing—Beijing has been China's center of government.

For much of China's history, the common people, especially the millions of peasants who farmed the land, lived in poverty. Few emperors attempted to improve the lot of the peasants, and many were cruel and harsh rulers. These days the powerful Communist government runs China from Beijing, where a peasant song, thousands of years old, is still sung:

When the sun rises, I go to work,
When the sun sets, I go to rest,
What use is the imperial power to me?

The Earliest Inhabitants

Nearly half a million years ago, long before Beijing became a city, people lived in the area's limestone caves. The people and the land both looked different then. The adult cave dwellers were short, standing about four-and-a-half or five feet tall. They knew how to chip stones and how to shape them into simple weapons and tools that the people used for hammering, scraping, and cutting. Dense forests covered much of northern China, where wild animals roamed.

The people gathered wild plants and hunted deer and other game. They probably caught and ate insects, frogs, turtles, birds, and other small creatures, too. But most of the time, they feasted on seeds, fruits, and nuts. They didn't grow their own food, nor did they have pottery or baskets to use as containers. But they may have stored seeds and nuts in bags made from animal skins.

During the winter, they probably wore clothing made from animal skins. They roasted their game, huddling around their fires to keep warm. When the weather was cold, the home fire was the center of their lives. The women probably stayed close to the caves, taking care of the children and tending the fire, while the men roamed the nearby forests, gathering food.

Scientists—mainly from Europe and North America—have provided most of what is known about these early peoples. The scientists studied fossilized skeletons that had been discovered in 1927 in the limestone caves near Beijing. At that time, scientists and other people called the city Peking (a variation of Beijing). As a result, the remains from the nearby caves were said to belong to the Peking people. Further studies have shown that these earliest residents of the Beijing area were members of a widespread early human species known as *Homo erectus*.

A Military Outpost

At the beginning of the Bronze Age, roughly 3,000 years ago, the site of what would become Beijing was a small settlement of people who hunted and raised livestock. The site lay on the main route between Mongolia's plains and the rich farmland to the south—an ideal spot for all kinds of trading activities.

Some of the settlers were craftspeople who worked bronze, clay, and wood into a variety of sellable goods. Other residents were merchants who bought and sold the things the craftspeople made. Still others were nobles who served the local ruler as hunters and warriors.

Many centuries later, by about 475 B.C., the site had grown in size and importance to became the capital of the Yen kingdom, one of China's small ancient realms. Yen leaders called their capital Chi and ruled from a central palace in the heart of the city.

Chi had a large population of soldiers, whose job was to defend the city from attacks by other kingdoms or by the Huns.

Fierce warriors, the Huns controlled Mongolia and other lands to the north.

Chi soldiers wore helmets in battle and protected themselves with shields. Their weapons included crossbows, bows and arrows, and a long-handled weapon with an ax blade and a dagger at the end. Some of the warriors fought from large horse-drawn chariots. Each chariot carried a driver, a lancer, and an archer.

When good men are in office, government is efficient, just as when the earth is fertile, plants flourish. —Confucius

A Royal Household

By this time, the ideas of Confucius, a Chinese philosopher, had gained some attention among the powerful. Confucianism stressed a strong moral code and encouraged societies to be strictly arranged into classes. Confucius also supported the idea of service to the emperor. Almost everyone in the Yen kingdom had a master, except the king, who was all powerful within his realm.

Yen kings inherited the kingdom from their fathers and passed it on to their sons. The king had one principal wife, who also came from a royal family, and many secondary wives called concubines. The king, his wife, and his concubines all lived in the royal palace.

The palace wasn't just one building. It was more like a bustling town within a town, with lavish dwellings, beautiful gardens, and impressive temples. Other members of the royal family also lived within the palace grounds. Most of these nobles were brothers, sisters, aunts, uncles, nieces, nephews, and cousins of the king. Together these nobles made up Yen's aristocracy, the kingdom's most important and powerful social class.

The palace had a social hierarchy. Lesser-ranking nobles served those of a higher rank, and commoners or slaves waited upon the lesser nobles. Many noblemen were army officers or ran the day-to-day affairs of the kingdom. Some aristocrats acted as the king's personal servants. Each rank was completely obedient to the rank above it.

Although the nobles worked, they were the only people in the kingdom who also had leisure time. Those in the military staged elaborate archery contests to develop and display their skills. Noble officials built temples where they offered sacrifices of food to the spirits of their royal ancestors. They also performed complicated rituals to celebrate marriages and other important events.

Peasants, Merchants, and Artisans

Commoners made up most of the Yen kingdom's population. They weren't as powerful as the nobles, and they weren't as powerless as the slaves.

Most commoners were poor farmers who lived outside the walls of the city, toiling to feed themselves and their families. But there were commoners inside the city, too. Some were artisans who made goods from wood, bronze, jade, pottery, and other materials for people of higher rank. Commoner merchants bought and sold these goods, sometimes amassing great wealth. Other commoners were cattle breeders who raised horses for the king's army.

All commoners paid taxes or faced

Weaving Silk

Women traditionally tackled all aspects of the manufacture of silk fabric—from tending the silkworms to weaving the strands into cloth.

severe punishment. The king and his officials decided how much each taxpayer owed. Peasants, who lived a slavelike life, were the poorest commoners. If a harvest was good, they could feed their families and pay their taxes, but if the harvest failed, they were the first to starve.

When the king and his officials wanted to build walls or to repair roads, they commanded peasants to do the work. In time of war, peasants were forced to be soldiers, defending the city from attack or venturing out to attack enemies. Women commoners usually spent their lives bearing and raising children and tending to household chores, either in their own homes or in the homes of someone higher in social rank.

A Slave's Life

The slaves were the least powerful people in the Yen kingdom. Their owners could do with them as they pleased. Slaveholders were sometimes even permitted to kill disobedient slaves.

Some people were slaves from birth because they were the children of slaves. The same people who owned their parents, owned them. Others became slaves as punishment for committing crimes or for offending someone of a higher rank. Offenders were sentenced to slavery for a certain period of time, perhaps a year or two. When they finished serving their sentences, they were no longer slaves. Still others were enemy prisoners whose captors forced them into slavery.

Many slaves spent their lives doing hard physical labor. Others worked

Cruel Choices

In times of famine, the poorest commoners sometimes survived by selling one or more of their children, usually daughters, as slaves. In some cases, the family was allowed to buy the child back when the famine had ended.

as servants, cooking meals for wealthy families, doing household chores, running errands, or taking care of livestock.

Slaves sometimes developed a loyalty to their owners. Some of them even served as bodyguards, accompanying their owners on journeys and protecting them from robbers or enemies.

Beautiful young women from poor families might catch the eye of a noble or even of the king and become a slave in his household. Powerful noblemen and kings could choose to make a slave woman into a concubine. Sometimes such women rose to great power. If a woman bore a son to the king, there was always the chance that her son might become the next emperor. If that happened, his mother became very important, and her relatives rose in status.

15

The Khitans and Yenjing

During the eighth and ninth centuries, nomads called the Khitans, a Mongol people, roamed the steppes (grasslands) far to the north of China. The Khitan way of life—which depended on hunting, fishing, and raising animals—required the people to move constantly as their need for food and shelter changed according to the seasons. But the Khitans sought to expand the lands under their control and eyed the fertile Chinese lands to the south. The Khitans invaded in the early tenth century, a period of instability for the Yen kingdom, and founded the Liao dynasty (family of rulers).

The Khitans built an imperial palace on the site of Chi and protected the city with 30-foot-high walls. Among the names given to the capital was Yenjing, which means "swallow capital," a reference to the swallows (small birds) that nested in wooden buildings in and around the site.

Although they lived among and ruled the Chinese from Yenjing, the Khitans kept their own society intact. They built a separate economy, maintained some nomadic customs, and developed their own political and military organizations. Khitan leaders, for example, were forbidden to work as civil servants, and Khitan nobles were punished for any interaction with the Chinese.

For more than 200 years, the Khitans successfully defended Yenjing against raiders from the south. Walls begun under the Yen kingdom also helped to slow the advance of northern invaders. But the site of Beijing still suffered the attacks of foreign, especially Mongol, armies.

Genghis Khan, Mongol emperor from A.D. 1167 to A.D.1227, in ceremonial dress.

How Long Was the Wall?

The Great Wall, which passed almost within sight of the city, stretched from the Bo Sea to the Gobi Desert, for a distance of about 4,200 miles. If a wall that long were built in United States, it would reach from Alaska to New York.

18

Walls and Invaders

Yen rulers had long been forcing slaves and peasants from Chi and the surrounding countryside to build huge stone walls along the kingdom's northern border and later around the city itself. The rulers of other small kingdoms in northern China also ordered walls built.

Wall building was backbreaking, exhausting work. Millions of huge stones had to be hauled up steep mountainsides. Half a million workers died of exhaustion, disease, or injuries before the walls were completed. Eventually joined together, the defensive barrier became known as the Great Wall of China.

Although the Great Wall made it harder for invaders to attack, it didn't keep them out. Conquerors, such as the Khitans, sometimes overpowered the defenders and forced their way through the gates of Beijing.

One of the most powerful invaders was a fierce Mongol commander named Genghis Khan, whose name meant "Emperor within the Seas." His empire extended from Russia to the borders of China, and his troops were the fiercest fighters Asia had ever seen. Skilled horsemen who fought from their saddles, the Mongols attacked several parts of China, including Beijing, in the 1200s.

Genghis spent his life in the vast open steppes of Asia and vowed that he would never live in a walled city like Beijing. He never did. In 1215 his troops burned the city. Genghis pushed on to other conquests.

In time the Mongol armies took control of China and founded the Yüan dynasty. By then Genghis Khan had died, but his grandson, Kublai Khan, became the new emperor.

> *This new city is of a form so perfectly square...that when a person...looks right forward, he can see the gate opposite to him on the other side of the city.* —Marco Polo

Life Under Kublai Khan

The Chinese viewed their culture as far superior to that of the Mongol conquerors or to that of any foreigners. The people of Beijing and of other Chinese cities knew how to make paper, gunpowder, and other important products. Chinese artists, poets, and writers produced outstanding works of art and literature.

These accomplishments impressed Kublai Khan, who became emperor in 1260. He decided to rebuild the capital, making the city the hub not only of China but also of an empire that included all of central Asia, much of the Middle East, and most of Russia. Kublai called the city Khanbalik (city of the Khan). The people called it Tatu, meaning "great capital."

Although Khanbalik was a splendid capital and trading center, it was not as rich as the port cities along China's eastern coast. They had easy ways to receive and move goods and were connected by the Grand Canal, an artificial waterway. Moreover, Khanbalik was a long way from the fertile rice paddies of the south. Kublai wanted his capital to be the empire's premier city, so he ordered the construction of a new canal that would link Khanbalik to China's river systems. Kublai also built a major, paved road that ran from Khanbalik to the southern end of the Grand Canal, more than 1,100 miles from the city. Within the capital, Chinese engineers dug several lakes. Because of these improvements, rice-filled barges from the south could sail up the canal right into the city's artificial lakes to unload their goods.

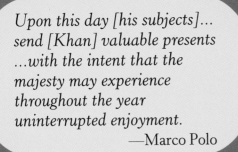

> *Upon this day [his subjects]... send [Khan] valuable presents ...with the intent that the majesty may experience throughout the year uninterrupted enjoyment.*
> —Marco Polo

A Man Named Marco

In 1275, during the reign of Kublai Khan, traders from Venice, an Italian port city, made their way to Khanbalik. The emperor's vast domain reached most of the way to Europe, and his road improvements eased European travel. Up until this time, few Europeans had visited China. The journey was too long, too dangerous, and too difficult.

In the Venetian trading party were Niccolò Polo, his brother Maffeo, and Niccolò's 20-year-old son Marco. Marco was amazed to see people in Khanbalik buying and selling things with paper money instead of with gold or silver coins. He was astounded that the Chinese used coal and oil for fuel. He could hardly believe the lavish gifts that were presented to the emperor by his subjects.

Kublai liked Marco and appointed him to be one of his assistants. Marco's job was to travel to other parts of China, find out what was happening, and report back to the emperor in Khanbalik.

After 19 years in China, Marco wanted to return to his Italian homeland, but he had become so valuable, the emperor didn't want to let him leave China. Finally, Kublai Khan was persuaded to let Marco go on an important mission to Persia (modern Iran). When Marco arrived in Persia, he received news that the emperor had died.

Marco went home to Venice. He wrote about his adventures in Khanbalik and in the other parts of Asia he had visited. He described a gift to Kublai Khan of more than 100,000 white horses. He wrote about seeing the Chinese using charcoal—he called it "black stones that burn"—to heat their houses and to cook their food. He said the emperor employed thousands of astrologers, who claimed they could predict wars and earthquakes by studying the stars. He wrote detailed accounts of the empire's paper money, which paid for the construction of roads and canals.

Marco told about all these marvels and many more in his book *Description of the World.* For several centuries, many Europeans scoffed at Marco Polo's stories and refused to believe him. Later travelers proved his reports to be true.

Forbidden City

After Kublai Khan died in 1294, his empire began to crumble as the Chinese people rebelled against Mongol rule. In 1368 a Chinese rebel commander named Chu Yüan-chang marched toward Khanbalik with an army of nearly 250,000 soldiers. The Mongol rulers abandoned the city and fled, ending the Yüan dynasty. Taking the name Hung-wu, the commander became the first of 16 emperors from the Ming dynasty.

After capturing Khanbalik, Hung-wu destroyed much of the Mongol city and set up his capital in Nanjing. Yung-lo, the third Ming emperor, moved the capital back to Beijing in 1402 and began restoring the magnificent city that Kublai Khan had built.

For 19 years, Yung-lo's crews labored. They rebuilt the city's walls and created a city within a city—a walled imperial palace with courtyards, gardens, temples, and luxurious living quarters. Around the palace, workers dug a huge moat and stocked it with fish. In 1421, when the work was completed, Yung-lo and his wives moved into the palace and officially made the city his new capital, giving it the name Beijing, meaning "northern capital."

Yung-lo was so powerful that he was treated like a god in human form. No one but the emperor, his wives, and their servants were allowed in the innermost parts of the palace. For that reason, the palace came to be called the Forbidden City. The commoners of Beijing lived outside the palace walls but within the walls of the city itself.

The Forbidden City included many artificial and natural water sources.

Curfew

Every night, a bell was rung to mark the beginning of the curfew, which meant that people were expected to go to their homes. At intervals throughout the night, the time was announced by the beating of a drum in a tower.

The Lives of Women

Like the rest of China, Beijing was strongly influenced by the ideas of Confucius. He believed that men of good moral character who respected their father and their emperor were the basis of a strong society. This point of view led to the idea that men were superior to women. As a result, life for women and girls in Beijing was often difficult and demeaning.

From the time they were born, girls were treated with less respect than anyone else in the family. They were expected to obey not only their fathers, but their brothers—even their younger brothers.

In times of famine, a poor family might sell one or more of the daughters into slavery and use the money to buy food. Girl babies who were too young to be sold were sometimes killed by their parents. Even if a girl survived, her father had total control over her life, including choosing whom she would marry.

> *Why must the feet be bound? To prevent barbarous running around.*
> —Yüan dynasty rhyme

In China at this time, small feet were considered a sign of female beauty. Many Chinese girls underwent the painful practice of foot binding, which prevented the bones of their feet from growing normally. Mothers would tightly wrap their daughters' feet in strips of cloth. Foot binding not only deformed the feet, but by adulthood many women could barely walk.

When a woman married, she was to obey her husband as she had her father. If she did not, her husband might beat her, and there was nothing she could do about it. If a couple went anywhere in public—a rare occasion—the wife was to walk 10 paces behind. Wives owned no property, received no education, and couldn't work outside their homes. Husbands could divorce their wives, but no matter how badly a wife was treated, she could not divorce her husband.

Secretly lock the postern gate. Restrict her to courtyard and garden. Then misfortune and intrigue will pass you by.
—traditional advice given to Chinese bridegrooms

Cheating

Participants in the mandarin exam had to be well versed in Confucian teachings. Some students avoided memorization by copying the classic writings onto their underclothes.

The Mandarin Exam

Being born into an important family wasn't the only way to become rich, powerful, or well respected in the imperial city of Beijing. Some of the most important Ming officials were scholars who had gained their authority by passing examinations.

Confucius first came up with the idea of testing potential government officials. These early exams were given only to the sons of nobles or of wealthy families. Those who passed the tests became members of an elite class of government officials known as mandarins.

Mandarins held important imperial positions. As symbols of their elite status, they wore richly embroidered clothes. To show the world that they had no need to work with their hands—something peasants and other commoners had to do—mandarins grew their fingernails long. Some fingernails were longer than the fingers themselves.

Eventually, the system was reformed to allow educated people from all walks of life to take the tests. When Beijing again became the capital in the fifteenth century, young men came from all over China to compete. Those with the highest scores took more tests, sitting for long hours in tiny cubicles. As the days of testing wore on, some competitors became exhausted or ill and could not finish. After the ordeal was over, those who had survived would relax together as they awaited the results. It became a tradition to fly kites after the examination.

29

These nineteenth-century engravings show the enduring popularity of Chinese kites *(right)* and board games *(below)*.

Kites and Games

In the Ming capital of Beijing, those who could afford leisure time flew kites, played cards or dominoes, and tried to defeat their opponents in chess. Kites had long been popular in China, coming in all shapes and sizes and attracting adults as well as children. Many brightly painted kites, made of rice paper and bamboo, had fancy tails. Others resembled birds with wings that flapped in the wind.

Other games, many of them with very long histories, were played throughout imperial Beijing. *Wei-chi*, a challenging board game, was rooted in military strategies and was a favorite with commanders and nobles. The game's purpose was not to kill or destroy the opponent's army but to surround and capture territory.

Many people enjoyed chess, a game based on warfare, as a pastime. Chess sets had carved game pieces that depicted generals, horsemen, infantry, elephants, cannons, and war chariots. A wide variety of card, dice, and domino games, including the domino game of mah-jongg, were favorites.

Sports were popular as well. One game, developed by warriors in the Han dynasty, was called *tsu-chiu* or kickball. Another age-old team sport was a tug-of-war game.

Offering Sacrifices

Chinese emperors were religious as well as political leaders. In fact, the people regarded the emperor as heaven's representative on earth. Every year, at the beginning of the farming season, the emperor led an early morning procession through the streets of Beijing to the Temple of Heaven. Outside the temple stood a huge altar, which the people of Beijing considered the center of the universe.

As the sun rose in the east, the emperor sacrificed a young bullock, amid the sounds of a sacred flute and the chanting of ceremonial singers. Along with the sacrifice, he offered prayers for an abundant harvest. It was the most important religious ceremony of the year.

From ancient times, the people of Beijing also prayed to the spirits of their ancestors. Emperors believed that their royal ancestors, although dead, could still bring good fortune to their descendants.

By the fifteenth century, religious rituals were an important part of life in Beijing. The city was dotted with many temples, plazas, and wide avenues that could be used for ceremonies and processions.

The Temple of Heaven was the most magnificent. It has been called the noblest example of religious architecture in China. Only the emperors and their households were permitted to offer sacrifices there.

Religion in Beijing

Over the centuries, Chinese beliefs blended Buddhism, Taoism, and the teachings of the ancient philosopher, Confucius. Buddhism, a religion that had originated in India, taught people to increase self-knowledge through meditation. Taoism arose in ancient China and held that people gain wisdom and health by conforming to the laws of nature. Confucius instructed people to practice honesty, bravery, and obedience to their leaders.

When People Got Sick

The Ming emperor Yung-lo not only wanted to preserve Beijing, he also wanted to preserve the knowledge of ancient Chinese practices that had been passed down through the centuries. He put hundreds of scholars to work writing a huge encyclopedia that would include ancient medical practices.

The remarkable encyclopedia listed nearly 2,000 kinds of drugs made from roots, leaves, bark, berries, animal products, and minerals. The book described more than 8,000 ways to use these herbal remedies.

The book also discussed acupuncture, an ancient medical technique of inserting needles into various parts of a patient's body to relieve pain. According to age-old Chinese beliefs, good health depends on an energy force known as *qi* that travels through the body along 14 distinct paths. Qi is partly active (yang) and partly passive (yin). If anything disturbs the flow of qi, the yin and yang elements get out of balance, and the person can become quite sick or experience great pain.

Acupuncture was a way to restore the proper flow of qi through a person's body. Skilled practitioners inserted the slender needles, which were seldom thicker than a human hair.

Tai Chi Chuan and the Art of Combat

According to some historians, the inspiration for Tai Chi Chuan, a form of Chinese martial arts, came when a Taoist priest of the Yüan dynasty watched a snake and a bird fight. As the bird attacked with its strong beak, the snake defended itself by carefully executing twists and turns. In time, the bird got tired and careless, and the snake was able to deliver a fatal blow. From watching these animals, the priest determined that aggressiveness can be bettered by patience and cunning.

Later martial arts specialists of the Ming dynasty developed the movements and principles of Tai Chi. Meaning "great ultimate fist," Tai Chi is a method of attack and defense as well as a form of mental and physical exercise.

Tai Chi masters taught students how to make slow, flowing movements; how to control breathing and maintain proper body position; and how to fight in armed and unarmed combat. These and other techniques not only benefited the muscles and bones but also reestablished the harmony between yin and yang. In Beijing practitioners of the art studied long and hard to perfect their postures, movements, and meditative skills.

Singers with Painted Faces

In 1644, during a period of political turmoil, an invading army from Manchuria (a region northeast of Beijing) swept down on the Ming capital, captured it, and established the Qing dynasty. The dynasty, sometimes also called the Manchu dynasty, lasted nearly three centuries.

During the Qing era, Beijing opera became hugely popular among ordinary Chinese. Based on earlier dramatic forms, Beijing opera combined music, dance, storytelling, painted faces, costumes, and acrobatics.

The operas told stories from ancient Chinese folklore or history. Some were about great warriors and their battles. Others presented legendary disputes among the gods or traditional love stories.

The actors, all of whom were men, sang in Mandarin, the dialect of the Chinese language spoken in the capital. Through pantomime, the actors revealed the emotions of the characters they played. When a character was angry, for example, the actor might whirl about the stage like a violent tornado. Sorrow might be represented by the actor wiping away imaginary tears. To show surprise, the actor might do a series of back flips.

Some actors achieved great fame, and many performed at the emperor's court theater in Beijing. In the 1700s and 1800s, the emperor allowed the actors to live, rehearse, and perform at the Summer Palace, which was located just outside the capital.

Each opera actor's face was painted with bold, striking designs in bright colors. Makeup, costumes, masks, and headdresses let the audience know what kind of person an actor was playing.

Gold dust on painted walkways,
half is scattering of stars, the
moss at the lodge by the pool,
a single swathe of green.
  — from *Peony Pavilion,*
  a famous Chinese opera

British troops stormed
the Summer Palace
during the Opium War.

The Empire Slowly Crumbles

Although the Manchus were foreigners, they had adopted Chinese ways. They expanded the trade network begun under the Ming emperors. From the very beginning of the dynasty's reign, Qing rulers saw the value of continuing and improving the making of fine porcelain. The imperial government established royal kilns (ovens) where master potters could exercise quality control and could try out new techniques. By the early 1700s, Qing wares had become a popular trade item with European merchants.

During the 1700s, Chinese trade in porcelain and other goods increased with Britain and other European nations. The Chinese, who looked down on the Europeans, bought few goods in return and limited trade to the port of Guangzhou.

The Europeans were intent on balancing and expanding trade with China. In the 1800s, the British began smuggling opium into China, where the drug was illegal and expensive. Nevertheless, many Chinese bought it and became addicted. The emperor's efforts in 1839 to abolish the trade resulted in the Opium War, which China lost. As a result of the defeat and of later treaties in the 1840s and 1850s, the Europeans were able to increase foreign shipping, to send in Christian missionaries, and to set up diplomatic offices in Beijing.

Meanwhile, the corrupt Qing dynasty weakened. The humiliating treatment of the Chinese by foreigners led to a series of anti-imperial rebellions from the mid-1800s to the early 1900s. By 1911 the Qing dynasty had ended, and the Republic of China was formally declared on February 12, 1912. A successful warlord named Yüan Shikai took over Beijing and installed himself as president.

41

So many deeds cry out to be done, and always urgently; time presses. Ten thousand years are too long, seize the day, seize the hour!
—Mao Zedong

An Occupied City

The early republic wasn't very stable. Several groups fought to gain control of the new government, which at that time was in Beijing. By 1927 a young general named Jiang Jieshi (Chiang Kai-shek) had taken charge. The next year, he moved the capital from Beijing to Nanjing and changed the old capital's name to Peiping.

Meanwhile, another young man—Mao Zedong—was gaining great popularity among China's peasants, who had suffered for centuries under one emperor after another. Mao was a founding member of the Chinese Communist Party, which vowed to bring land reform and equal rights to the peasants.

Both Jiang and Mao had strong followings, and their armies clashed throughout the 1930s. In the meantime, World War II (1939–1945) broke out. Japan occupied northeastern China, including Peiping, in 1941. During the war, the armies of Jiang and Mao fought the Japanese.

By the time the war ended in 1945, peasants had swelled Mao's army into a formidable force. With aid from the United States, Jiang took over Peiping and other northern cities. Civil war erupted in 1946 and continued until 1949, when the Communists were able to gain control. They occupied Peiping, changing its name back to Beijing. Residents lined the streets to watch Mao's victorious army march into the city unopposed, carrying their supplies in trucks and on pack mules.

In October 1949, Beijing again became the capital of China. Speaking to a great crowd of people near the Forbidden City in Tiananmen Square, Mao proclaimed the founding of the People's Republic of China. As head of the Communist Party, Mao became as powerful as any emperor and made sweeping changes that affected the lives of all Chinese.

Communist troops often marched through Beijing's streets.

The Walls Come Down

*T*he Communist government changed the way Beijing looked and the way its people lived. New orders put residents to work building houses and factories. Other crews widened the city's streets. Government workers tore down the huge walls that had long surrounded most of Beijing, creating a huge ditch that encircled the city. In the ditch's place went tracks to make a subway line. A later subway line connected the center of the city to the western suburbs. For very little money, residents of Beijing could travel quickly from one side of the city to the other.

After the old city walls had been removed, the government extended Beijing's boundaries far into the nearby countryside. A portion of the Great Wall of China landed within the expanded city limits.

Workers also restored and remodeled Tiananmen Square, the vast plaza in the heart of the capital, and preserved the historic buildings and gardens of the Forbidden City. For the first time, ordinary Chinese citizens could visit the site and see how the emperors had lived. The Communist government also turned many old temples into museums and built many small gardens and parks, where residents could relax, walk, or practice Tai Chi Chuan.

Mao's government outlawed many ancient customs and traditions. Laws, for example, prohibited discrimination based on gender and banned foot binding and forced marriages. Yet the government also imposed controls on many social, economic, and cultural aspects of Chinese life.

Cyclists pedal down a Beijing thoroughfare.

Events in Tiananmen Square

By the late 1980s, students and other residents of Beijing were seeking ways to express their feeling that the Communist Party had too much control over their lives. The Chinese government operated businesses, set prices for goods, and decided what people could publish. It legislated how many children people could have and where people could travel. But openly criticizing the party could cost people their jobs. Some critics could be sent to prison or even be executed.

Even some government officials were speaking out in favor of greater freedoms. Hu Yaobang, the party's secretary general since 1980, had been fired from his post in 1987 for expressing such views. Many Chinese considered him a hero.

When Hu died on April 15, 1989, student leaders organized a mass demonstration in his memory. On April 18, several thousand people gathered in Tiananmen Square to honor him and to call for reforms. Within days the number of demonstrators in the square approached 100,000.

On May 13, about 3,000 of the demonstrators started a hunger strike, refusing to eat unless the government enacted democratic reforms. Hundreds of thousands stayed in the square to support them. On May 16, Zhao Ziyang, Hu's replacement, promised that steps would be taken to build a more democratic government. He urged the protesters to leave. The students refused.

The next day, more than a million Chinese converged on the square. Beijing's residents blocked troops sent to disperse the crowd. Most of the demonstration's supporters eventually left. About 20,000 demonstrators remained.

The government dispatched about 100,000 soldiers in armored vehicles to suppress what the party was calling a student rebellion. During the early morning of June 4, the soldiers entered the square and began firing at demonstrators, most of whom were unarmed. International human-rights groups and the Chinese government disagree on the number of persons killed. The estimates range from 300 to 3,000.

Protesters crowded Tiananmen Square in the spring of 1989.

Rivers of Bicycles

Beijing has more bicycles than any urban area in the world. Very few people in the city can afford to own and drive cars, but bike traffic is heavy. Estimates suggest that four million bicycles crowd the city streets, and the number is growing steadily. With so many people using bicycles, it's not surprising to see bicycle parking lots and bicycle repair shops everywhere. All bicycles must be licensed and equipped with a bell.

People on foot have to be careful when they cross busy thoroughfares to avoid being hit by a bicycle. During the morning, when millions of people are on their way to work or school, the streets are like rivers of bikes. Instead of the blaring of automobile horns, the air is filled with the "ching-ching" of bicycle bells.

No matter what the weather, children ride bikes to school, and adults ride them to work. When it rains, businesspeople, students, shoppers, and shopkeepers wear ponchos as they pedal.

Bikes not only transport people, they also haul goods. Bikes piled high with crates of live chickens are used like wheelbarrows, with the owner walking alongside and balancing the bike. Street vendors pedal pushcart bikes built with two wheels in front. Merchandise is carried and displayed in a case mounted above the front wheels. Some cyclists earn a living pedaling large tricycles called "pedicabs" that can carry one, two, or even three passengers at a time.

Bicyclists dominate the streets in downtown Beijing. Cyclists routinely lock their bikes so they won't be stolen.

Flying Pigeon

In Beijing it is common to see an adult riding a bicycle carrying one or two small children as passengers. The most popular brands of bicycles are the Flying Pigeon, the Forever, the Phoenix, and the Favorite.

51

Language and School

Schoolchildren in Beijing study hard, learning to read and write Mandarin Chinese. The official Chinese language has no alphabet. Instead each word has its own separate picture or character, and there are about 50,000 different characters. By fourth grade, Beijing schoolchildren, using brush and ink, have learned to write the characters for about 2,000 words.

Reading and writing Chinese is so difficult that it takes a lifetime to become really good at it. Many words use only two or three simple brush strokes, but some require as many as 20. Students who are planning to go on to college need to be able to write about 5,000 words.

Children in Beijing start nursery school as young as three years old. Daily activities include exercises in a playground

Reading and Writing

China has long respected education. But before 1949, only 2 out of every 10 Chinese knew how to read and write because most Chinese never went to school. These days almost everyone has at least six years of schooling. Yet of China's more than one billion people, 20 percent—roughly 200 million—still aren't literate.

(below). At six or seven, they begin their primary education. For the first few years, they spend most of their time studying reading, writing, and math. In math classes, students learn to calculate with an abacus, an ancient Chinese device that uses beads to count and to quickly solve arithmetic problems.

Twice a day, children in primary schools take a break for exercises intended to rest their eyes. The children, seated at their desks, close their eyes and use their fingers to massage their foreheads, eyebrows, cheekbones, and noses.

In the upper grades of primary school, students continue to study reading, writing, and math, but other subjects are added, including geography, history, physical education, and nature study. After nine years of education, many children leave school and go to work. Others continue their secondary education to prepare for college or for jobs as skilled workers.

Eating in Beijing

Marco Polo let the world know about Beijing's fine food. During his stay in the capital in the 1200s, he would have eaten dishes that originated with the Mongols. Because they were herders and not farmers, the Mongols introduced recipes that included meat, wild game, mare's milk, and yogurt. Dishes coming from the south used plenty of vegetables and rice.

Mongolian fire pot is a popular specialty in Beijing. The waiter brings to the table plates of raw mutton and vegetables and a special cooking device—a small copper stove topped by a doughnut-shaped kettle. The kettle contains a hot, clear broth. The diners pick up the meat and vegetables with chopsticks and hold them in the bubbling broth until they are cooked. Then the diners dip the cooked foods in spicy sauces.

The city's most famous dish is Beijing duck, one of the world's tastiest and most elaborate meals. It takes at least 24 hours to prepare and is served in three separate courses. In the first course, the roasted skin of the duck is chopped up, mixed with scallions, and rolled with a sweet dark sauce in a thin pancake. Next comes the duck meat, which cooks have carefully cut into thin slices to be served with bamboo slivers or bean sprouts. The third course is a soup in which fresh cabbage is simmered in stock made from the duck bones.

Although people in Beijing eat rice, many residents prefer foods prepared from wheat, which grows better than rice does in the climate of northern China. Noodles, dumplings, and other foods made from wheat flour are especially popular, as are fried bean curd and foods cooked with water chestnuts.

Chinese locals enjoy dumplings and other delicacies from outdoor vendors.

New Year!

For four days every winter, factories, offices, and schools close while the people of Beijing celebrate Chinese New Year, the country's most important annual celebration. Residents decorate their houses, dress in new clothes, and make elaborate meals to mark the new year.

In the streets, people shoot off long strings of firecrackers, and young men wearing brightly colored costumes dance to the sound of gongs, cymbals, and drums. Costumed men and boys clown around on stilts, and troupes of acrobats perform at the Great Hall of the People.

Chinese New Year is also called Spring Festival. It begins sometime between January 20 and February 20. The exact

Midnight brings fireworks to a new year celebration near the Drum Tower in Beijing.

Don't Sweep Away Good Luck

Each year, as the new year approaches, people are busy sweeping, cleaning, and scrubbing the places where they live and work. After the festival begins, the sweeping must stop. Some people say anyone who uses a broom when there is so much good luck around might accidentally sweep some of it away.

date is based on the traditional Chinese lunar (moon-based) calendar, which starts the year on the second new moon after the beginning of winter.

For centuries the holiday was a time for people to honor and pray to their ancestors. The Chinese believed that if they offered food and drink to departed family members, the spirits of their ancestors would help them in the coming year. Although the holiday has lost much of its religious significance, it is still a time when families celebrate together. Grandparents, parents, aunts, uncles, cousins, and children all come together for huge family banquets. On the first day of the new year, adults give red and gold envelopes containing money to their children, grandchildren, nieces, and nephews.

57

Life Goes On

For thousands of years, Beijing has seen governments come and go. Most residents don't much care that they live in the capital of the largest Communist country in the world. Like their ancestors, they are too busy simply earning a living.

Economic reforms are raising the standard of living. Under Mao, the Communists preached against privately owned businesses and brought all industries under state control. Mao died in 1976, and these days millions of Chinese are eager to engage in private enterprise. To some degree, the Chinese government is encouraging them.

Residents of Beijing are opening businesses in partnership with companies from all over the world. McDonald's and Kentucky Fried Chicken are just two of the U.S. fast-food chains that have opened restaurants in Beijing.

It may seem as if China has been a Communist country for a long time and that reforms have been slow in coming. But for the people of Beijing—whose city can trace its beginnings back 3,000 years—half a century isn't so long a time. In the long history of Beijing, half a century is almost nothing.

Ancient architecture meets skyscrapers in Beijing's cityscape.

Beijing Timeline

100,000 B.C.–A.D. 905 **Ancient Beijing**	**100,000 B.C.**	*Homo sapiens* and Paleolithic culture evident in China
	10,000 B.C.	Early Neolithic cultures
	2000 B.C.	Beijing founded as trading center
	1600–1050 B.C.	Shang dynasty
	1050–256 B.C.	Zhou dynasty
	479 B.C.	Death of Confucius
	400–200 B.C.	Beijing made capital of Yen kingdom
	206 B.C.–A.D. 220	Han dynasty
	A.D. 105	First mention of paper in China
	A.D. 653	Earliest surviving code of laws
	A.D. 868	Oldest existing book published
	A.D. 905	Khitans invade
A.D. 1200–A.D. 1937 **Imperial Beijing**	**A.D. 1215**	Troops of Genghis Khan burn walled Beijing
	A.D. 1260	Kublai Khan becomes emperor
	LATE 1200S A.D.	Kublai Khan builds city in its present form
	A.D. 1275	Marco Polo visits
	A.D. 1294	Kublai Khan dies
	A.D. 1368	Capital moves to Nanjing
	A.D. 1421	Yung-lo returns capital to Beijing

A.D. 1644	Qing rulers build temples and palaces
1700s A.D.	Chinese trade porcelain wares with European nations
1800s A.D.	British smuggle opium into China
A.D. 1839	Opium War is fought and lost by China
A.D. 1860	French and British diplomats allowed in city
A.D. 1900	Anti-foreigner Boxers kill German diplomat in city
A.D. 1912	Last Qing emperor removed from power by Yüan Shikai
A.D. 1919	Students protest Japan's influence on China
A.D. 1928	Jiang Jieshi takes control of Beijing from warlords
A.D. 1937	Japanese defeat Chinese defenders of Beijing

A.D. 1945–
Modern Beijing

A.D. 1945	Chinese Nationalist army recaptures city from Japanese
A.D. 1949	Chinese Communists, under Mao Zedong, take over city
A.D. 1966	Cultural Revolution begins
A.D. 1976	End of Cultural Revolution; earthquake kills about 240,000 in city; Mao dies
A.D. 1989	Hundreds of students killed during demonstration in Tiananmen Square
A.D. 1995	Beijing hosts UN conference on women
A.D. 1997	Deng Xioping, Mao's successor, dies

Books About China and Beijing

Cotter, Alden R. *China Past-China Future*. Danbury, CT: Franklin Watts, 1994.

Feinstein, Stephen C. *China in Pictures*. Minneapolis: Lerner Publications Company, 1989.

Forman, Werner and Cottie A. Burland. *The Travels of Marco Polo*. Toronto: McGraw-Hill Book Co., 1970.

Gao, Qian. *West to East: A Young Girl's Journey to China*. San Francisco: China Books and Periodicals, 1996.

A Guide to Beijing. Lincolnwood, IL: Passport Books, 1987.

Haskins, Jim. *Count Your Way through China*. Minneapolis: Carolrhoda Books, Inc., 1987.

Jiang, Ji. *Red Scarf Girl: A Memoir of the Cultural Revolution*. New York: HarperCollins, 1997.

Kent, Deborah. *Beijing*. New York: Children's Press, 1996.

Lattimore, Owen and Eleanor Lattimore. *Silks, Spices, and Empire*. New York: Delacorte Press, 1968.

Ling Yu. *Cooking the Chinese Way*. Minneapolis: Lerner Publications Company, 1982.

McLenighan, Valjean. *China, A History to 1949*. Danbury, CT: Children's Press, 1983.

Metil, Luana and Jace Townsend. *The Story of Karate*. Minneapolis: Lerner Publications Company, 1995.

Peng, Wenlan. *Living in Peking*. Hove, England: Wayland Publishers Ltd., 1981.

Pitkänen, Matti. *The Children of China*. Minneapolis: Carolrhoda Books, Inc., 1990.

Piyun, Hu. ed. *Historical Photos of Old Beijing*. Beijing: Beijing Publishing House, 1995.

Reid, Howard and Michael Croucher. *The Fighting Arts*. New York: Simon & Schuster, 1983.

Schneider, Mical. *Between the Dragon and the Eagle*. Minneapolis: Carolrhoda Books, Inc., 1996.

Teague, Ken. *Growing Up in Ancient China*. Mahwah, NJ: Troll, 1994.

Thompson, Peggy. *Kids in China*. New York: HarperCollins, 1991.

Index

abacus, 53
acupuncture, 34
artisans, 12
Asia, 19, 20, 23
Beijing opera, 38
bicycles, 50
Bo Sea, 18
Bronze Age, 8
Buddhism, 33
Chi, 4, 9, 16, 19
Chiang Kai-shek. *See* Jiang Jieshi
Chinese Communist Party, 43, 47
Chinese New Year, 56–57
Chu Yüan-chang. See Hung-wu
civil war, 43
Communists, 4, 44, 58
Confucianism, 11
Confucius, 11, 26, 29, 33
Description of the World, 23
education, 52–53
Europe, 6
Europeans, 22, 41
food, 54
foot binding, 27, 44
Forbidden City, 24, 43, 44
fuel, 22–23
Genghis Khan, 19

Gobi Desert, 18
Grand Canal, 21
Great Hall of the People, 56
Great Wall of China, 18–19, 44
Guangzhou, 41
Han dynasty, 31
Homo erectus, 6
housing, 49
Hung-wu, 24
Huns, 9
hutongs, 49
Hu Yaobang, 47
Japan, 43
Jiang Jieshi, 43
Kublai Khan, 19, 20–21, 24
Khanbalik, 4, 20, 24
Khitans, 16–17, 19
leisure time, 31
Liao dynasty, 16
lunar calendar, 57
mah-jongg, 31
Manchu dynasty. *See* Qing dynasty
Manchuria, 38
Mandarin Chinese, 38, 52
mandarins, 29
Mao Zedong, 43, 58
martial arts, 36
Middle East, 20

Ming dynasty, 24, 29, 31, 34, 36, 41
Mongolia, 4, 8–9
Mongols, 4, 16–17, 19, 20, 24, 54
Nanjing, 24, 43
nomads, 16
North America, 6
Opium War, 40–41
peasants, 13
Peiping, 4, 43
Peking, 4, 6
People's Republic of China, 43
Persia, 23
pinfangs, 49
Polo, Maffeo, 22
Polo, Marco, 22, 54
Polo, Niccolò, 22
population, 49
private enterprise, 58
qi, 35
Qing dynasty, 38, 41
religious rituals, 32
Republic of China, 41
royal household, 11
Russia, 19–20
slaves, 14–15
Spring Festival. *See* Chinese New Year
steppes, 16
Summer Palace, 38
swallow capital, 17

Tai Chi Chuan, 36, 44
Taoism, 33
Tatu, 20
Temple of Heaven, 32
Tiananmen Square, 43–44, 47
tsu-chiu, 31
Venice, 22
wei-chi, 31
women, lives of, 26–27
yang, 35
Yen kingdom, 9, 11, 12, 14
Yenjing, 4, 16
yin, 35
Yüan dynasty, 19, 24, 36
Yüan Shikai, 41
Yung-lo, 24, 34
Zhao Ziyang, 47

About the Author and Illustrator

Robert F. Baldwin of Newcastle, Maine, and Des Moines, Iowa, has traveled extensively in Asia and visited Beijing in 1996. A veteran writer of newspaper and magazine articles, he is also author of *New England Whaler* in the American Pastfinder series published by Lerner Publications Company. When not writing, Baldwin works as an actor and storyteller.

Ray Webb of Woodstock, England, studied art and design at Birmingham Polytechnic in Birmingham, England. A specialist in historical and scientific subjects, his work has been published in Great Britain, the Netherlands, Germany, and the United States. He still finds time to teach young people interested in becoming illustrators.

Acknowledgments

For quoted material: p. 4, old peasant song relayed orally to author while in Beijing; p. 10, Archie J. Bahm. *The Heart of Confucius.* (Berkeley; CA: Asian Humanities Press, 1992); pp. 20, 22, Manuel Komroff. *Travels of Marco Polo.* (New York: Horace Liveright, 1926); pp. 26, 27, Julie Checkoway. *Little Sister.* (New York: Viking, 1996); p. 39, Stephen Owen, ed., *An Anthology of Chinese Literature.* (New York: W. W. Norton and Company, 1996); p. 42, Jean Chesneaux. *China: The People's Republic, 1949–1976.* (New York: Pantheon Books, 1977).
For photographs and art reproductions: Ancient Art & Architecture Collection Ltd., p. 18; Stock Montage, Inc., pp. 22–23, 30–31 (inset); © John P. Stevens/ Ancient Art & Architecture Collection Ltd., pp. 24–25; Corbis-Bettmann, pp. 30–31, 42–43; Corel, pp. 38–39, 50–51 (both), 52–53; © Tony Stone Images/George Hunter, pp. 44–45; Reuters/Edward Nachtrieb/Archive Photos, p. 46; © Andrew E. Cook, pp. 54–55; Reuters/Corbis-Bettmann, pp. 56–57; © Andrew Holbrooke/ The Stock Market, pp. 58–59. Cover: © Andrew Holbrooke/The Stock Market.